Block

LIFESHOCKS
OUT OF THE BLUE

{ LEARNING FROM YOUR
LIFE'S EXPERIENCES

ANN MCMASTER, M.A., L.P.C

The author of this book does not dispense medical or psychological advice or prescribe the use of any technique as a form of treatment for physical, mental, emotional, spiritual, or medical problems without the advice of a physician, or a qualified psychologist, either directly or indirectly. The intent of the author is only to offer information of a general, educational nature to help you in your quest for emotional and spiritual well-being. In the event you use any of the information in this book for yourself, which is your constitutional right, the author and publisher assume no responsibility for your actions.

The events related in this manuscript, including conversations that occurred, have been re-created to the best recollection of the author, some situations have been modified, compressed, or expanded; and the names and identifying details of certain individuals have been changed for confidentiality purposes.

ISBN:1503146804
ISBN-13 9781503146808

Blade

There is no event in your life

through which Life is not coming

to awaken you to your highest

and most noble self.

Dr. K. Bradford Brown

Co-founder of The More To Life Program

Quote

DEDICATION

This book is dedicated to Dr. Kenneth Bradford Brown for his fierce devotion to the sanctity of truth, and personally for never giving up on me

&

to Dr. Wesley Roy Whitten for his incisive attunement to The Moment, magnetizing it for us all, and personally for saying the right thing at the right time to change my life.

APPRECIATIONS

My most sincere thanks to Peter Kiss for, kindly and insistently, keeping the idea for this book in front of my face; to the U.S. Board of the More To Life program for entrusting me to write it; to Dr. Anne Brown for giving me her blessing; to William Holt, my business partner, for his YES to the time it has taken; to my support partner, Diana Makens, who believed in me and kept me on purpose; to Bill Boothe, my forever friend, beta reader, context savant, for his astute insights and encouragement; to Jenny Meadows, editor extraordinaire, who understands the context of the More To Life program as well as my intent; to all my other beta readers – Kay Gilreath, Steve Waddill, Rhonda Schlatter, Peter Kiss for noticing the gaps; lastly to Wilene Dunn – patient friend, insistent agent, making it all happen. Special thanks to my family, all of them, for being not just family, but pathmates – my son-in-law, Troy, grandkids Hayleigh and Chase, who keep the heart-fires burning. And especially to my daughter, Rebecca, who evokes the best in me, as she does everyone else.

CONTENTS:

control.

Blake

LIFESHOCKS - OUT OF THE BLUE

Foreword

In May 1982, my life changed direction. I had no premonition, no warning. Several friends and I flew from Texas to California to play in the sunshine and to attend a little weekend course that would earn us continuing education units for our psychotherapy licenses – nothing more. It was supposed to be a fun few days.

I began the course in the secure knowledge that my life was working. I was successful in my practice, my relationships were solid and supportive, my self-esteem was high. There were no troubling issues in my life. The timing could not have been more perfect – get this little program out of the way, and we could go back to having fun in the sun.

The first morning of the course I watched a woman transform from a mousey victim to a regal warrior. Person after person shed painful burdens they had unknowingly carried for years. Unconscious behaviors that undermined their lives were brought to light and dealt with consciously and compassionately. I was stupefied. I had not realized that kind of deep transformation was possible with so many people in such a short amount of time. I wanted that for myself, so I engaged rather than observed. One of the major skills taught that weekend—fundamental to the whole More To Life program, and the subject of this book—is the tool for uncovering unconscious motivation for behavior that sabotages the best within us, including our hopes and dreams. It was through this technique that I discovered a belief I had put in place at the age of 9 that had been buried in my psyche, and which I had no clue was there. In my mind, the image is crystal clear – standing in the doorway as my parents were leaving for the evening, and hearing my dad say, "You're in charge. If anything happens to any of the kids, it'll be your fault." Whether he actually said that or not, I have no idea. All I know is, that is what I heard, or what I interpreted he meant, and it's the imprint I lived with for the next 28 years.

The consequence for assuming the liability for my siblings resulted in feeling burdened, anxious about their welfare, fearful of my capability to manage their lives, and resentful of my role in the family as the eldest of four – and later five, then six, then seven, then eight. Too many lives to manage, not enough wherewithal to be competent – loads of self-doubt as an undercurrent throughout my life. I lived with that incessant runnel of fear – not having a smidgen of a clue that there was another option. From the outside, even from the inside, my life looked successful. I was healthy, respected in my profession, money in the bank, close family connections, and lots of good, solid friends. Letting go of that fear made my life immensely more relaxed and at peace.

Knowing my dad from the advantage of maturity, I doubt he meant those words the way I took them. The upside of that subterranean message resulted in a career as a psychotherapist, coach, trainer, mentor, consultant. Go figure!

And all along, life was sending me course-correcting wake-ups, requiring me to set boundaries, take responsibility for the quality of my own life, to trust myself, to trust the journeys of others, and to have faith in the ultimate goodness of life. This book is also about that.

PURPOSE OF THIS BOOK

In the early 1980s, based on material from a number of sources, including their experiences as Episcopal priests and Dr. K. Bradford Brown's experience as a PhD Clinical Psychologist, he and Dr. W. Roy Whitten created a training program that enabled people to make fundamental changes in their lives. Their premise is that being awake to reality – the reality of our own essence, the reality of our relationships with the people and places in our lives, and the reality of the moment and circumstance in which we find ourselves – has everything to do with the quality of our lives. That way of living is very different from living in an automatic, reactive pattern. Even though the unconscious, habitual patterns of behavior rarely, if ever, deliver the result we intended, we can be at a loss as to how to change those behaviors. I used to tell Life, "Just speak in plain English!" … so I could understand how to stop repeating life patterns that I didn't like, didn't understand, and didn't know how to reverse or get out of.

What is learned in this program, now called More To Life, formerly known as The Life Training, is how to notice the messages we get from … whatever you want to call it … Life, God, Allah, The Force, Universal Light, Higher Power. The purpose of these messages is to wake us up so we can transform those self-sabotaging behaviors and set a path that is more congruent with our essence. Brad and Roy called these messages, these wake-ups from Life, *Lifeshocks*. They come out of the blue as gifts to shock us out of our reactivity or to compel us to become even more of who we are when we are at our best. Our task is to notice them, discern the message, proactively respond, and be grateful for the opportunity to make a difference – in ourselves, in others, and in the world. This opportunity for waking up, for making conscious changes, is a fundamental premise of the program. Tools and skills for managing our response to these Lifeshocks are what are offered. Other programs offer other ways to have similar effects. I personally found this way to be quick, efficient, and deeply effective for myself and for many others worldwide.

This book has been written to demystify and clarify the concept of Lifeshocks and to present the Clarity Process as a methodology for understanding and deciphering the messages inherent in Lifeshocks. Hopefully it will be illuminating for those who have participated in the More To Life program, as well as for those who have not.

Chapter 1

Lifeshock – What Is That?

Out of the blue, without pre-knowledge, without our consent, unexpected things happen. The way we know things happen is because we see them with our eyes, hear them with our ears, smell them with our nose, taste them in our mouth, or feel them on our skin. Or some combination of all of the above. They are actual empirical happenings, not a label or title for an experience. This sudden, un-asked-for thing that happens, perceived via our senses, is called a Lifeshock.

Those times in our lives when we change course, grow up, wake up, lighten up, transform, become more of who we really are, see others more clearly, have more understanding of what is really going on – those times are precipitated by a Lifeshock – a gift from Life. Lifeshocks happen at specific moments and are a vehicle of evolution – inviting us to wake up in three ways: more self-awareness, more awareness of the full reality of others, and more awareness of the reality of the larger context in which we are currently living – whether that context is our family, our workplace, the judicial system, religion, our time in history, the world's resources – in essence, the more global Reality.

Lifeshocks are proffered to us via empirical reality – incoming data delivered via our senses of sight, sound, smell, taste, touch – and, when we are really in tune, via our sixth sense (which has our normal five senses as its base). Lifeshocks are not realizations, assumptions, considerations, predictions, or conclusions. They are Real Reality, outside our normal/personal reality, an offering to upgrade our personal reality so we can be in sync with Real Reality. When we are in sync with Real Reality, we put aside our little personal reality, sometimes called The Way We Think It Is or The Way We Think It Should Be, sometimes called ego.

When we are in sync with Real Reality, we are more able to maximize the best in ourselves, more able to relate to others empoweringly, and more able to accurately assess the lay of the land – all of which enable us to be more creative, proactive, and contributive.

Lifeshocks happen, they are out of our control, and they are Real. They are devoted to our awakening, to our evolution. If we ignore the little Lifeshocks or pretend they didn't happen, they just get bigger and louder. And if we continue to ignore them, they crank up the volume until we cannot NOT get them!

Lifeshocks are a moment in time when something happens. They don't have to be major. They can be an instant that feels like a niggling question mark, for example.

Calvin

Henry and Harriet were parents who had a personal reality that their children simply did not do drugs. Their egos allowed no other reality. There was a disparity between their reality and the Real Reality.

Lifeshock – Their son Calvin as he's going out the door says, "I'm going over to Bert's." Neither Henry nor Harriet knew Bert or had ever heard Calvin mention him before. They ignored that Lifeshock, folding it conveniently into their internal paradigm.

Lifeshock – Calvin's six-week report card: Days Absent 8; GPA C- (down from A-). Henry and Harriet ignored these two new Lifeshocks, writing them off as teenage slump, nothing to worry about, he'll come around.

Lifeshock: Calvin's skin: gray-ish.

Lifeshock: A neighbor friend asked Harriet, "What's the matter with Calvin? Is he doing drugs?" Henry and Harriet got mad at the neighbor for even suggesting that a member of their family would use drugs ... still committed to their version of Calvin, asleep to the Real Calvin.

Lifeshock: Out of the blue, Calvin in full seizure, body jerking and straining.

Lifeshock: Henry and Harriet waiting outside the emergency room, the doctor saying, "We pumped his stomach. He overdosed on PCP."

Henry and Harriet were totally shocked, didn't even know what PCP was. It wasn't until later, after they had set aside their insulated perception of their family, that they were able to see the Lifeshocks they had missed because they had been so intent on seeing Calvin the way they wanted him to be.

What Calvin had wanted all along was to be seen by his parents ... really seen for his unique being. Being 'good' (acting like he 'should' act or how he was expected to act) hadn't awakened them to who Calvin was, and being 'bad' almost killed him. But at last his parents let go of their reality (little 'r' reality) of Calvin and saw him much more clearly – the Real Calvin. They were then there for him in a much more tangible way.

Justine
Justine had been a teacher for more than twenty years, having received glowing commendations from all her previous principals. James, the new principal, was a bully, used to getting his way because of his past experiences, his physical size, and his position at the school. Justine had a personal history of caving in, acquiescing to the imperiousness of others (beginning with Mom). She got one Lifeshock after another, caving in further each time, until James lied one time too many.

The Lifeshock: Out of the blue, James is explaining to the panel that was hearing his complaint: "All of Justine's previous principals also had problems with her."

That Lifeshock was the one that finally awakened Justine, who promptly went and got her record of glowing commendations for the last twenty years. She hired an attorney, did her homework on all James' accusations from the beginning, and started recording his posturing. She transformed from meek and self-doubting to committed and self-assured. That part of her was there all along, accessed as an athlete and in other places where she felt confident, but not accessed when faced with anyone who reminded her of her perception of her mother during her childhood. (And there can be a vast difference between our perception of people and the Reality of who they are.)

Alex

Alex and Dave were salesmen for a furniture warehouse, a company whose job was to find retail outlets for furniture manufacturers.

Lifeshock: Out of the blue, "Our customer decided to hire their own sales force."

Lifeshock: Sales Manager says, "Our first quarter sales are down 30%."

Lifeshock: At happy hour after work, Alex, Dave, and two other co-workers are hanging out. One of them says, "Yeah, Sam and I are looking for another job."

Alex had already started feeling uneasy about his position, but that last Lifeshock was the one that turned the corner for him. He started looking at his company's profitability, and whether or not his job was viable, given the reality of being a manufacturer's representative in the furniture business in this current time and in his part of the country. He talked to the

Sales Manager, researched his industry, and made a decision.

Dave received the same Lifeshocks as Alex and didn't know what to do, so he didn't do anything. A later Lifeshock ("We're letting you go.") got him moving, more out of fear than of proactivity.

The whole "movie" of an event isn't a Lifeshock – the movie is full of Lifeshocks. Choose the most impactful moment as the Lifeshock to freeze-frame.

Calvin's drug addiction is not a Lifeshock. It's an issue that has many Lifeshocks within it. Hearing the doctor say, "He overdosed on PCP" is the Lifeshock with the most impact.

James' lying is not a Lifeshock. Hearing James say, "All of Justine's previous principals also had problems with her" is the Lifeshock.

Being aware of a downturn in business is not a Lifeshock. Being told, "Our first quarter sales are down 30%" is one of the Lifeshocks.

In all of these examples, the Lifeshocks have a common characteristic: a specific moment in time, like a freeze-frame of a video. A Lifeshock is not the story or a label for the situation, but one impactful instant within the video/story when something specific was seen/heard/etc.

In a worst-case scenario, ignoring, discounting, being ignorant of Lifeshocks can literally end our lives. Ask the tsunami victims who didn't notice the water being sucked away from the beach, or a driver who wasn't paying attention to the erratic movement of another car.

Pretending a Lifeshock didn't happen leads us into deeper separation from ourselves, from others, and from Real Reality, farther from actualizing our goodness, and isolating us even more from those we love or from whom we want approval or recognition.

Every couple I've ever worked with, when one of them had had an affair, the signs were there, ignored by the other partner. In fact, the Lifeshocks were there way before the affair was even begun.

Pinpointing the exact Lifeshock is life-enhancing, because intertwined with each Lifeshock is the mechanism for releasing us to the best in ourselves, to our ability to love and be loved, to the latent creativity inherent in each moment.

Lifeshocks are irrefutably, inexorably, and relentlessly about waking us up to two things – that which is Truth (aka big 'R' Reality) and that which is False (aka Illusion). That which is now on offer instead of that with which we've grown comfortable. That which is now awake instead of that which was asleep. Connected instead of isolated. Free instead of imprisoned. Serene / agonizing, compassionate / judgmental, creative / bored, alive / existential death, heaven / hell.

Lifeshocks are the signposts to coming home, illuminating our self-deception and offering the fulfillment of our destiny as spiritual beings having a human experience.

Chapter 2

How Do Lifeshocks Work?

The body processes billions of pieces of information every moment – all the incoming data from all our senses, all the adjustments in the sympathetic and parasympathetic systems, maintaining the body's normal functioning – keeping the heart beating, eyes blinking, processing and distributing food/nutrients, and everything else it does so miraculously. This amount of information is way more than the conscious mind can hold in awareness.

Thankfully, we have the reticular activating system (RAS), part of the mammalian brain located in the brain stem. It is a loose network of neurons and neural fibers that contributes to the control of sleep, walking, sex, eating, elimination, and, most importantly – the control of consciousness. In order to consciously focus attention on something, the RAS dampens the effect of stimuli that are non-essential to our current mission, so we don't get sidetracked by overloaded senses.

For example, the mall near me has a perpetually crowded game room right at my usual entrance. My RAS is so focused on getting to my favorite store that it diminishes the cacophony of the game room to such an extent that the discordant sounds barely register in my awareness. If my RAS didn't perform normally, my auditory nerves might be swamped to such a degree that I would be overwhelmed by the loudness of the input, and my forward progress would be stymied. As it is, I am not even slightly deterred.

The RAS is important to know about because it focuses on creating whatever is currently held in the mind – whether consciously or unconsciously held. This ability to edit out information which is non-essential to the current program held in the RAS is both a blessing and a curse, depending on whether the current program is aware and intentional or fear-based. More on this later.

Our RAS is also instinctual and designed to react to the slightest threat to our survival. It is always searching for any relevant information that will avoid danger and ensure our continuance. It is the mechanism by which a friend of mine avoided being decapitated in a collision with a truck. She ducked under the dashboard just before the roof of her car was sheared off by the truck. No time to think, only react. And she survived without a scratch, no conscious volition involved. Her car died, though – no Reticular Activating System deployed.

This instinct for survival has allowed us to continue our species over the eons, sometimes against the odds. Imagine early mankind, rudimentary weapons, saber-toothed tigers and other predators looking at human beings as a food source. Those of us with slow reactions were the ones whose genes rarely got passed to the next generation. Those of us with the quickest reactions were the ones most likely to breed the future. Bottom line: Those reactions tend to be knee-jerk and embedded in our instinct for survival.

A half step up from those instinctual reactions are those reactions preceded by thought, mostly unconscious thought. Today, even though there are so very few saber-toothed tigers from which to protect ourselves, we still have that instinct to protect and preserve our lives ... surviving a potentially scary, unknown future as detailed daily on the evening news. Robbery, rape, murder, economic downturns and downsizing, war, road rage, fears of all kinds – fear of failure, of being exposed, of public speaking, of deaths of all kinds (of people, through divorce/separation, being fired/let go), of moving, of changes (even 'good' ones), of traffic jams, of financial pressures, of never being loved – the list is endless.

The adrenalin produced by escaping saber-toothed tigers is an amped-up version of the daily rush experienced when we narrowly avoid an accident or feel any of the myriad fears faced in any given day. As fast-paced as the world is, it's easy to get caught up in the epinephrine rush.

What does the RAS have to do with Lifeshocks? While the RAS is focused on a specific mission, it can ignore Lifeshocks that it deems irrelevant to the current mission. That usually results in the Lifeshocks getting louder and stronger until the RAS accommodates the information it can no longer tune out.

What makes our seemingly instantaneous reactions so acute and critical is that Lifeshocks are, by their very nature, unpredictable, out of the blue. So we are constantly adjusting to an ever-changing scenario, while attempting to establish some predictability in our lives. However, Life does not seem to be interested in predictability – except the prediction that, sooner or later, things will change, whether we want that change or not.

Choosing what happens to us and to those we love, or hate, is not within our domain. Just as we didn't get to choose whether or not a predator wandered into our territory, we still don't get to choose whether or not a tsunami wipes out our settlement, or there's an oil crisis, or our child gets cancer. Out of the blue, things happen – over which we have no say.

As if that weren't demeaning enough, we also have no say in our reaction. It's built in and practically instantaneous – for the sake of preserving the life we have or think we should have. And it's one more thing over which we have no control.

So no control over Lifeshocks (things that happen to us) and no control over how we react (instinct for survival). Great! What DO we have control over?

Well, we have control over two things: how long we stay in our reaction, and what we choose to do after that. And when we make choices about going forward more realistically, there are no guarantees that these more-reality-based choices will succeed. All we are ever guaranteed is that, as long as we are alive, we will be given the gift of more Lifeshocks – communiqués from Life. And when we get really, really sensitive to Lifeshocks, our own heartbeat becomes that gift – *ka-thump, ka-thump* (*wake up, wake up*).

Let's start with the reactions to Lifeshocks. There are two kinds of reactions, which are generally experienced as either positive or negative. We can tell we've had a positive reaction to a Lifeshock because we feel happy, satisfied, uplifted – changed in some way for the better.

When we label Lifeshocks 'positive,' that really means we like what happened, they meet or exceed our expectations, we are in the flow with Reality – maybe even grateful for the Lifeshock. There is nothing to do but enjoy the moment. Revel in the good feelings. We have basically just said "YES" to whatever happened – "YES" to the Lifeshock, "YES" to how we are feeling, "YES" to the way we feel so connected to our goodness and to others, "YES" to how we fit into the bigger scheme of things. Enjoy!

It is only a matter of time before a Lifeshock happens that we don't like – one that we wish hadn't happened, one that we Really Don't Want, or one we don't know how to handle. That will be a Lifeshock to which we are likely to say "NO." And we can tell we are saying "NO" to the Lifeshock because we feel some form of fear or hurt or upset; i.e., angry, sad, pissed off, scared, worried, depressed. In those cases we will feel lonely – isolated from our own goodness, separated from others, believing we are different/outcast/alienated from the flow of life that others seem to enjoy.

We can stay in our NO to the Lifeshock for extraordinary amounts of time. I met a woman whose husband died. She was still grieving his death, wearing black, bemoaning the loss of her love, talking about how unfair life was, how empty her life was without him in it. I assumed it was a fairly recent event. Actually, her husband had died almost forty years previously, when she was in her late 20s, and those forty years had passed her by, while she was still saying NO to the reality of her husband's death.

Fundamentally, when stuck in our NO to a Lifeshock, we do whatever we can to ignore Reality or pretend it doesn't exist … or we attempt to reverse it in some way, force it to change to something we can live with or to something we think we have to have.

Our NO is expressed in many ways:
- Blithely continuing as if the fantasy of our relationship hadn't been exposed
- Pretending that someone's promotion over us didn't hurt
- Withdrawing into ourselves
- Refusing to speak up
- Turning suffering/sadness into an art form
- Giving up – on our dreams, on our relationships, on hope
- Living in resignation about our lot in life
- Stopping believing in ourselves or that things can really change

- Whining/complaining about what's happening
- Rising above it all with pseudo-enlightenment/self-delusion of superiority ("I didn't really want it anyway")

Then, of course, there is the other tactic – do whatever we need to do to change reality into that which we have decided we are owed, or want, or think we have to have. That's when we are likely to experiment with the following:

- Reactively glaring at/shouting at/spanking/beating a child for misbehaving
- Vehemently bad-mouthing politicians for some vote we disagree with
- Railing against someone or something (e.g., the justice system for unfair treatment)
- Hurting someone intentionally (from physical abuse to 'the silent treatment') to make them change
- Begging/pleading for someone/something to change
- Pushing any and all 'guilt buttons'
- Bullying/overriding people
- Bargaining with God/Life/The Force; e.g., "If you'll just grant this one request, I'll be good forever."

The list of manipulations is endless, varied, and extraordinarily creative – and then habituated – even though none of it seems to guarantee success. But hope springs eternal in the human breast, and occasionally something works, so we seek to figure out the formula for predictable success.

Unfortunately, or fortunately, depending upon our viewpoint, Lifeshocks remain unaffected by our attempts to control them – to change/limit/make them happen or make them un-happen. And Life never gives up on us, offering us one Lifeshock after another – bigger, more impactful, more pungent, more undeniable – until our NO crumbles and our YES emerges.

Example:
My sister died in 1970 at the age of almost 24. There were a gazillion Lifeshocks during the ten years that I watched her die from von Recklinghausen's Disease. My story line was "They will come up with a cure." And that's what I held onto, even as I watched her health deteriorate month by month. In order to maintain the fiction of my NO in the face of contrary evidence (i.e., Lifeshocks inviting me to the reality of her decline), I saw her less and less as she got worse and worse. The night before she died, I saw her struggle for breath, a rattle in her chest. I could hardly stand to be there. Even at her funeral, I shed not one tear. There was a corner of my mind that shut off that reality. Instead I focused on being there for my family (there were six other younger siblings), keeping up a good front.

Many years later, I was relating a dream to a friend of mine about Lazarus coming out of the tomb. My friend (knowing about my sister) asked me if I knew of anyone who had died. I said, "No." There was silence in the room (my mother also happened to be present). Then I heard my mother's wail. I folded with the onslaught of years of withheld anguish, and through my throat came all the bottled-up grief sounds that had never been expressed for my sister.

My YES to the fact of her dying released a lot of fear/energy that I had spent repressing the reality of her death. Before my YES to her death, I had no pictures of her in my house, and I never talked about her. After my YES to her death, I had more of a sense of being connected to her, appreciating her place in my life, remembering our good times and our fights with equal appreciation, cherishing my Susie stories. Our pictures of when we were ages 3 and 1 now have a prominent place in my home. My regret was how much time I wasted in avoiding the truth, and how I did not have the connection I wish I had had with her as she made her transition from living to dying. She gave me plenty of opportunity. Now, instead of pretending she never existed in order to keep my NO alive, I have my YES and my gratitude for her and for all I've learned from her life, as well as from her death.

Chapter 3

How the Mind Works

In and of themselves, Lifeshocks are simply events that happen – neither positive nor negative. They simply are. The Lifeshocks we like we consider good-positive-wonderful. The Lifeshocks we don't like we call bad-negative-terrible.

The proof that they are neither positive nor negative is when two or more people experience the same Lifeshock and have dissimilar reactions. The proof is the same person having the same Lifeshock at different times and experiencing different reactions.

For example: a baby's smile might be considered positive by one person and negative by another; a 92 on a test could result in a happy dance by one person and be a downer for another; someone not saying hello back to me could ruin the rest of my day, but on a good day, the same scenario might result in feeling compassion for someone who's just preoccupied or having a bad day.

Lifeshocks are real, tangible, out of the blue, and out of our control. The problem is that our reactions are also real, tangible, and almost instantaneous. Therefore, the natural conclusion is that the Lifeshocks cause our reactions. I.e., I behave this way only because *that* happened. If *that* hadn't happened, I wouldn't have reacted that way. There doesn't seem to be any other plausible possibility.

Lifeshock (Reality)		Reaction (Feelings)
sensory input	⟶	physical sensations

If that were really true, every time something happened, everyone would react the same way. And every time the same thing happened to me, I would react the same way. However, every time you say, "I love you," I don't react the same way.

Why is that? What is obvious and conscious is what happens and how we feel about it. However, what goes unnoticed and is unconscious is our interpretation, our mindtalk, our spin on the Lifeshock. The mindtalk is real, but it is not tangible or discernible through any of our senses, and it takes place within nanoseconds. Mindtalk attempts to explain the unexplainable. It has opinions, beliefs, accusations, conclusions, judgments, expectations and demands, hypotheses (only right ones, of course), and loads of predictions about everything and everybody. It makes decisions about us, about 'them' and about 'How It Is.' And we live with those decisions thereafter, even though we don't realize we made them.

There is a difference between the mind that is creative, innovative, resourceful, imaginative, artistic, unfettered, unattached to a specific outcome, and the reactive mind that is contaminated by anxiety/fear, relying on deeply rooted matrices of tenets designed to ensure our safety or avoid anything that might be painful.

This methodology is about uncovering the reactive mind, releasing it, so that our creative mind can take us forward.

In Real Reality, the Lifeshock happens, our mind interprets whatever happened (Reality) through our filters of gender, age, experience (Mindtalk), thereby determining our Reaction and what we feel.

In Real Reality, the diagram looks like this: (bottom)

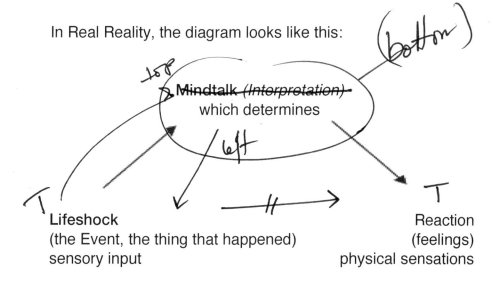

top

Mindtalk *(Interpretation)*
which determines

left

Lifeshock
(the Event, the thing that happened)
sensory input

Reaction
(feelings)
physical sensations

Lifeshocks happen. How I react to the Lifeshock depends upon my interpretation. If I interpret the Lifeshock as something that meets or positively exceeds what I'm expecting will or should happen, then I like the Lifeshock. I am happy, satisfied, loving, experiencing other 'up' feelings. However, if the Lifeshock falls short of what I think should happen, then I don't like the Lifeshock. I am hurt, upset, pissed off, sad, scared, experiencing other 'down' feelings.

The degree of my up-ness or down-ness perfectly correlates to the degree of variance with what I expected or demanded. For instance, if I expected you to meet me at the airport, and I see you right where I expected you to be, then you've met my expectation, and I'm either happy about that or neutral. If, however, I was really tired from the trip, and I've looked at my watch for the third time and noticed that you are now forty-five minutes late, you have not met my expectation big-time, and I am pissed off. The more tired I am, the more pissed-off I'm likely to get. The bigger the difference between what I want and what I get, the more exaggerated the upset.

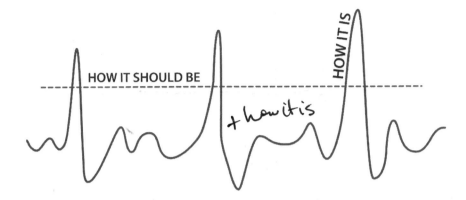

You may not meet my expectation because I haven't said I have one. I may not even know I have an expectation until you don't meet it or exceed it. All is excellent fodder for Lifeshocks to wake us up and be more aware of who we are, who others are, and how It Really Is. They expose our unconscious demands of how I should be, you should be, and It should be.

Example:

I'm living my life, all is well, I am content, everything is unfolding as expected. I'm in San Jose, California, in a training room. A woman is standing tall, without a microphone, able to be heard by everyone in the room. She says, "I am worth being seen." Previously her chest was concave, her shoulders were curved around her heart, and she could not be heard by anyone, even when speaking into a microphone. The change was so stark. The Lifeshocks for me were the straightness of her backbone and the clarity of her voice. My reaction was an immediate release of tears, tears of admiration for her. I felt evoked and inspired. I had a YES to that Lifeshock. And I wanted that kind of transformation in my life and for others. If she can do That, so can I. So can others.

Example:

I'm in the middle of the Kalahari, Botswana, with my new man. We've seen no one for days, only animals. It's our third night out, and I see him walking from the back of the vehicle with a bottle of wine in his hand. My immediate reaction is rigidity in my body. What takes me a while to catch is my mindtalk: "He's going to get drunk, I'm in the middle of nowhere with nowhere to go, there are wild animals all around us, he won't be able to protect me, I can't protect myself from him, this is an unsafe/dangerous place to be. I'm dead and no one will ever know. I should have known better. Men just can't be trusted. I can't be trusted to choose well. It's gonna get ugly."

He sees my face and stiff body – Lifeshock for him – which he interprets accurately. He says, "Ann, I'm not your dad, and I'm not your former boyfriend." That is a Lifeshock back to me, which short-circuits my reaction to the Lifeshock of the bottle of wine.

Example:

When my boss was anxious, he looked for somebody to blame. The more I demanded internally that he stop doing that, the more righteously steamed I became, which made working there more and more unbearable. Once I got the reality of the way he behaved when he was anxious, I started documenting the things he said. Then when he started his blaming routine, I would show him what I had documented. Seeing his own words on paper was a Lifeshock for him. He soon stopped blaming me. When I was able to see his behavior as his way of dealing with uncertainty, I quit taking it personally.

Example:

I worked with a woman who was not only a visionary, but a true strategist as well – an unusual combination. Unfortunately she kept running into the company culture that was steeped in "How It's Always Been." Her frustration level was off the charts, trying to implement improvements that would have increased the bottom line and stopped financial leaks. Her insistence that they listen to her only increased their deafness. There were many Lifeshocks during that time, but the one that changed her life happened during a meeting. She was presenting her statistics evidencing the necessity for change, and someone with no data said, "Don't worry, it'll happen." The second one was when the leader of the group, said, "OK, next on our agenda" … and went on to another topic, and her report was given no more deliberation. She ended up leaving – a relief to everyone, especially her. She let go of her demand that they be accountable to Reality, they let go of their demand that she stop shaking the trees. I have always wondered if they implemented her strategies after she left. That's often how that dynamic plays out.

That's what lifeshocks are – a Wake Up from the grist of our lives, delivered via our senses, inviting us to update our mental map of who we are Now, who others are Now, and how the situation is Now. Our ability to discern Reality, which is ever unfolding in front of us, determines the quality of our lives.

OK, Now what? Yes there are lifeshocks galore in every part of my life. What do I do with them? How can I use them in a conscious way to get into alignment with myself, with those around me, and with every moment of my life?

Read on!

Chapter 4

Getting to the Mindtalk

On the one hand, it is not mandatory to do anything with any Lifeshock. Most people don't. It is OK to live our lives following the unconscious, fear-driven dictates of our reactive mind. That mindtalk sounds like it is safe-guarding our best interests, working to keep us out of trouble or from getting hurt, and to get us what we want and where we want to go. It also sounds hauntingly familiar and rather normal.

On the other hand, it's also imprisoning, keeping us from living our lives joyfully and freely. We are either judging ourselves and others to be more or less than we really are, or we are righteously proclaiming that we know what should and shouldn't happen in our world, declaring an omniscience that we don't really have. We turn our wants and dreams into 'have to's,' as if we have no real choice, forfeiting our freedom. We make decisions that are meant to keep us safe, but which become our prison, robbing us of that which makes us whole.

Fundamentally we become a façade of ourselves, acting in ways that are contrary to who we are when we are at our best. The fear-based decisions likely made sense at the time, and maybe they worked back then, but mostly we were too young and inexperienced to be able to separate our internal fiction from Real Reality. When we are surrounded by others who consistently believe and act the same way, or who repeat behavior from which we need to protect ourselves, those beliefs and conclusions become hard-wired, cemented in by fear and hurt. And in that process we sacrifice our essential goodness, without realizing the price we are paying.

Example:

I met a physician on a plane. After we had been chatting a while, he started unraveling his doctor façade, talking about the lack of fulfillment he was experiencing, even while he knew that realistically there was nothing unfulfilled in his life. He loved his wife and kids, loved his career, had two really nice homes, and was financially secure. He was tall, handsome, rich, and athletic. He had it all and couldn't understand the emptiness he felt. When we delved further, the emptiness had started when he was a quarterback in college.

The Lifeshock he remembered was a time right after a game in which he was the star player, when his father turned away from him, without any clap on the back, no words of praise, no acknowledgment.

His reaction was the hole he felt in his chest, which never got filled.

His mindtalk was:

> "No matter what I do, I don't measure up.
> "My dad doesn't approve of me and never will.
> "I lack whatever it takes to make him proud of me.
> "I have to keep trying, keep proving to him that I'm worthwhile.
> "I'm missing something.
> "I don't know what it is.
> "So whatever I'm missing can never get fixed.
> "I'm never gonna win here. Not really.
> "It's hopeless for me."

Then the physician realized that the 'hole in his chest' had actually been there way before his college days, never receiving praise from his dad for any of his many accomplishments … still there to this day, wanting his father's approval. Once he realized what was causing him to suffer so much 'unfulfillment' in such a fulfilled life, he realized that his father 'praised' him by giving him a roof over his head, food in his belly, and a superb education. Also he had never asked his dad if he was proud of him. He had just assumed his dad wasn't because his dad didn't do what he thought a dad would do if a dad was proud of his son – i.e., clap on the back, praise, acknowledgment.

Example:
I have had the good fortune to lead some trainings in federal and state prisons. In one of these facilities was a gang member who shared that, at the age of 12, he knew his step-father, a macho drunk, was sexually abusing his two little sisters.

The Lifeshock that changed his life was seeing his little sister crying brokenly, for the third time.

He felt sick to his stomach, scared in his gut.

His mindtalk was:

>"I can't do anything.
>"He (the step-father) is going to kill me.
>"He hates me.
>"I'm no good anyway.
>"I can't even protect my sisters.
>"I have to get out of here.
>"I can't make it on the streets on my own.
>"I'm weak and powerless.
>"The only safe harbor is to become a gang member.
>"They will protect me.
>"If I don't join a gang, I'll die."

His decision to join a gang at 12 might have saved his life. The Lifeshocks were real, his fear was valid. What he hadn't realized was that his mindtalk was all lies. Those lies became ingrained, habituated to such a degree that later Lifeshocks were viewed through his haze of beliefs about being weak and powerless, thus having to prove he wasn't weak and powerless by doing violent acts to others.

Those ingrained beliefs can never be disproved enough. The reactive mind remembers all our failures and disgraces. They are like little whispers in the ear, "Yeah, no matter what happens, you know you are a schmuck. You might have everyone else fooled, but don't forget . . . . . . "

Example:
One of the major Lifeshocks about Susie's death was seeing a black body bag being wheeled through the front door on a gurney.
I felt shocked and immobilized.
My mindtalk was:

>"This isn't happening.
>"She can't be dead.
>"I have to make this un-happen.
>"This isn't right.
>"This doesn't happen in my family.
>"I didn't stop it.
>"I should have known what to do.
>"This is happening way too fast.
>"I need to slow things down.
>"I can't handle all this.
>"Because I'm incompetent and stupid.
>"I have to pretend this never happened."

The Clarity Process

In the More To Life program is a process called the Clarity Process, which is aptly named because it brings clarity to our lives as it clears away the debris, the haze through which we live when we are incarcerated by the lies of our reactive mind. Lifeshocks hold the key to our claiming more of who we are and reclaiming the bits that we have unknowingly sequestered.

The Clarity Process
1. Re-experience the Lifeshock and breathe into your feelings
2. Listen to your Mindtalk.
3. Verify: True – False – Don't Know
4. Tell the truth about the Lifeshock
5. Choose what now to do and how to be
6. Visualize yourself doing and being it

Begin the Clarity Process by accessing a Lifeshock, any Lifeshock. Zero in on the moment with the most physical impact on your body. Imagine that you are searching for a specific frame in a video of the event. Rewind the video to a place where you are at home in your own skin – plugging all your senses into the experience as though it is happening right now, noting what you are seeing, hearing, smelling, tasting, touching, and what you are feeling in your body. Steep yourself in those physical sensations. Roll the video forward, still being immersed in your experience, until you feel a physical impact in your body. Freeze on that frame of the video and breathe into your experience, allowing more and more of your feelings and emotions to bubble up. It sometimes helps to put your hand over the place in your body where you are feeling the most impact. You can also magnify feelings by breathing, giving them more life. (Breath=life; no breath=death)

Because feelings and emotions are predicated on mindtalk, if you take a moment to listen, they will lead you directly to your mindtalk. So while you are immersed in the Lifeshock and feeling your feelings (this is key), tune in to what your mind is telling you.

There are three subjects to explore – accusations, demands, and predictions. And there are three lenses through which to view each of those subjects – myself, others, and Life.

Accusations are judgmental fears and bitter epithets about myself, about other people, and Life. They sound like:
I am/others are fat, stupid, ugly, mean, not good enough, worthless, useless, pathetic, a failure, invisible, unlovable, don't matter, don't belong, different (in a bad way), selfish, cruel, hard-hearted, vicious, wrong, loser, evil, Life's hard, unfair, not worth the trouble, etc.

Demands attempt to disprove the accusations. They include words like *have to, should, ought, need, must,* and sound like:
I/others have to make this right, have to stop, have to win, have to behave, should have known better, shouldn't do that. People should be good − not bad, children shouldn't be starving, I need to make sure this gets done by five o'clock, I/others ought to always tell the truth, must never hurt anyone's feelings, must strive to always do best, Life should be harmonious and peaceful.

Predictions sound like:
I'll never get it together, he'll never change, it's all downhill from here, it's always going to be crappy, I'll always be the one who gets picked on, she'll always be mean, I'm going to get in trouble if I do this, I'll get fired, nobody will ever love me, it's too late to do anything different, no (future) relationship will ever be as good as this (last) one, Life will be hard, lonely, empty.

The reactive mind not only has accusations, demands, predictions, beliefs, judgments, conclusions, and dire warnings, it also loves to share them. It can't seem to stop itself. If your mindtalk seems to dry up after a few statements, there are ways to stimulate it, encourage it to spill more beans.

Ask about meanings, using phrases like "If X happens, then it means _____ (fill in the blank)."

E.g.: If Bob refused to unload the dishwasher, that means he doesn't love me; if he doesn't love me, that means he's cruel and a liar, and I've been duped again; if I've been duped again, that means I'm just a naïve bird-brain and he's a con man.

E.g.: If my boss doesn't give me the difficult work, it means he doesn't trust me; if he doesn't trust me by now, that means he's stupid; if he's stupid, that means I'm screwed; if I'm screwed already, that means I'm out of a job; if I don't get it right next time, it means I'm a failure, and I'll never have a job I really want, which means I'm a loser.

To get more predictions, use "If that's so, then I/Others/Life will . . . ."

E.g.: If we don't get this job, then we'll go out of business; if we go out of business, then we'll go broke; if we go broke, then we'll have to sell the house; if we sell the house, then we'll have to live on the street; if we live on the street, then we'll end up cold and alone and homeless.

E.g.: If she doesn't love me, then we'll end up divorced; if we end up divorced, then the family will break up; if the family breaks up, then we'll all live isolated lives; if we are all living isolated lives, then Life will be lonely and sad and pathetic.

There is also a way to combine accusations and demands so that they generate more accusations and demands. You can start from either end of the generator diagram below.

E.g.: *(demand)* I have to be perfect, or else I won't be lovable *(accusation), and if I'm not lovable, then I have to be what others want me to be, or else no one will love me, so I have to be good, or else they'll leave me, so I have to pretend everything is OK with me, or else I'll be all alone.*

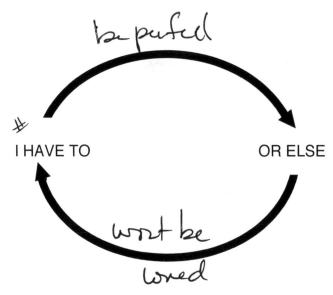

be perfect

I HAVE TO   OR ELSE

won't be
loved

E.g.: (*accusation*) I am not lovable, so (*demand*) I have to be perfect … and so on, around and around the generator.

Another trick the mind plays is to ask questions for which there is always an assumed underlying accusation or demand.
E.g.: *Why me?* The underlying assumed demand is: *This shouldn't be happening to me.*
E.g.: *How can I ever handle this?* The underlying assumed accusation is: *I can't handle this.*
E.g.: *What's wrong with you?* The underlying assumed accusation is: *There's something wrong with you.*

When processing, look for the assumed statement underlying a question.

It's often helpful to get someone else to facilitate the Clarity Process with you. Speaking your mindtalk out loud, with closed eyes, while your facilitator is writing it down, makes it easy to stay inside the Lifeshock moment, which is key to catching all the mindtalk. If there is a lag in accessing the mindtalk, they can ask questions (*And if that happens? Or else? And then you have to ___?*) about accusations, demands, predictions, assumed answers, meanings.

There are at least two ways to go through the Clarity Process solo. Some use a recorder, which makes it easy to keep the eyes closed, which makes it easier to stay inside the Lifeshock's moment of impact.

Others, like me, can write in my journal while I'm deep into my feelings, one piece of mindtalk per line. I've found I can cry and write at the same time. I've also noticed that when I'm angry and writing mindtalk I can practically read my writing from the reverse side of the page. When I run dry of mindtalk, I plug myself back into the Lifeshock moment, feel my feelings fully, and see if there is any more mindtalk. Sometimes it helps to switch my focus to me or to others or to how Life is going to be in the future.

I will know I am complete with this part of the process when I feel relief from the impact of the Lifeshock. Fundamentally, I will have opened the zip file of the unexpressed experience, and pressed it out. That relieves the imprisoned stress that had been contained within my body. The body wasn't meant to hold stress, so the effect of this part of the process is relief, a healing of an emotional wound.

And there is more. Once the trapped energy has been released, we are no longer entranced by beliefs we didn't know we had.

OK.   (*fix   italics.*)

Sometimes I feel crummy, and I don't know why. In that case, I rewind the video of my life back to when I was feeling easy in my body, then move the video slowly forward to the frame where I started feeling dis-ease. Then I can find the Lifeshock and breathe more life into that moment, expand my feelings, and listen to my mindtalk.

By the way, sometimes the feeling and/or a belief is so strong and so familiar, we can ride it back to a series of Lifeshocks that happened much earlier in time. So a current Lifeshock can actually stimulate previous memories of similar mental wounds and transderivate us back to when it all began. Our hindsight can then see the recurring matrix of mindtalk and how it has shaped our lives.

Chapter 5

Verifying

After the Lifeshock moment has been completely re-experienced, including all five senses and our feelings, and after all the mindtalk has been exposed, finally it is time to examine it from an objective point of view, from outside the Lifeshock moment – verify what is real, what is not, what is true, what is lie, what is something about which we don't truly know the answer.

There is a maxim that states, "Know the truth, and the truth will set you free." If we don't feel free, it's because we are not telling ourselves the truth. In my experience, telling myself the truth is essential for a quality life. Telling someone else the truth is more nebulous. Sometimes it is more compassionate, the higher option, not to tell someone else the truth. There are no specific guidelines about when to withhold the truth and when not to. The bigger question is whether or not it serves a higher truth – about ourselves, about someone else, or about a specific situation. Fundamentally, if I know the truth, then I can decide how best to go forward.

Most important is that WE know the truth about what we have been telling ourselves. What has our mind made up? Its job is to make sense of the mercurial unpredictability of life, to keep us out of harm's way … any harm. Basically, it is not that creative. Mindtalk relies on well-worn grooves, and much of it has been passed down from previous generations, or deepened by personal/familial tragedy, or is a polarization of our interpretation of the lives of others (I'll NEVER be like my parents).

Verification is a litmus test of reality, separating truth from fiction. There are three possible options for verifying reality –

saying what's True, False, or Don't Know about each piece of mindtalk. Each statement, on its own, is either True as it stands, or it is False, or it is something about which I Don't Know. The shorthand version is T, F, DK.

Tips for verifying:

- Feelings are always T. If I feel a feeling, I truly feel it, period.

- If the Lifeshock is that someone said, "I hate you," it's true they said it, it's likely true they meant it at the time, not necessarily true they meant it really, so that part would be either a T or a DK.

- If I failed to achieve something, it's true I failed to achieve it. But if my mind turns it into I AM a failure, that's a statement about my BEING and it's F. No one IS a 'failure' – as in, across the board, full stop, no exceptions, totally a failure in every way. No one. However, if I am determined to believe that it's T, I will ignore any success I might have and focus only on those incidents that prove I am right about being a failure. And I will be committed to a lie about myself, for which I will pay by losing my freedom to be creative and productive.

- All demands about how I (or someone else) have to be or what I have to do are F. Every demand I make on myself leaves me without choice, impotent, a slave to my own demands. There are always options. Every demand I make on someone else infers that they are without choice, a slave to my demands about their life, and those demands are therefore F.

- The 'shoulds' are a special-case F. They are the ultimate expression of omniscience. They state that "I know" how I, you, and Life should be. Really? Who made me the Knower of All Knowings? And it is soooo very tempting to pretend that "I Know" – especially when I am scared of not knowing. The trouble is that that pretense robs me of trust/faith in myself, in others, and in Life. That's a very big sacrifice to make for a pretense. The bigger issue about 'shoulds' is when the statement is something along the lines of *Children should not be sexually molested by anyone, ever.* That statement is easy to believe by most of us. However, children ARE being sexually molested – every day. So we can make a stand on This Shouldn't Happen – picket, march, bitch, complain, whine, carry on. Our demand that It Shouldn't Happen changes nothing. We are in opposition to the real Way It IS. And the real Way It IS supersedes our opposition – every time. Which renders us impotent, because we can't change what has already happened. It's not that it should happen; it's just that it's useless to rail against the Way It IS. *Children should not be sexually molested by anyone, ever* – F. *I don't want children to be molested by anyone, ever* – T, because that's what I really want. And when I know the truth and am free of my demands, then I'm also free to make choices about what I'll do/how I'll be with whatever is happening that I don't like.

- Generalizations, like *all men are ego-driven, all women are back-stabbers* – all F, because it's not all men, or all women, or all anything all the time.

- 'Always' and 'never' are dead giveaways – F. Even if it has always been like that in my experience, it's still not true everywhere always. 'Always' and 'never' are words that obliterate the possibility of something different, which isn't reality.

- Any statement about the future is a DK. Even if I have a very high probability of a certain outcome, the Real Truth is I don't know how it will come out for sure.

- Statements about what someone else thinks, if they haven't directly said what they think, are also DKs. Sometimes people, when angry or hurt, say things they don't mean, so even then it can be a DK.

- Look for the judgments and the shoulds beneath some of the truths. E.g., *I was laid off.* – T. Underneath that truth likely lurks a statement like *It shouldn't have happened* – F. If I don't notice that mindtalk and verify it, it will only keep me positioned in an alternate universe until I wake up and get that it happened … and now what?

Continuing with the mindtalk from the last chapter, let's verify what is T, F, and DK.

The physician's Lifeshock and mindtalk:

Lifeshock: his father turning away from him

Reaction/Feelings: hole in his chest, resignation

Mindtalk:

No matter what I do, I don't measure up (F)

He took his father's lack of praise and made an assumption that his father didn't think he measured up. By most people's standards, he far exceeded the measuring stick. Bottom line: It's really his own version of whether or not he measures up to his own standards that will set him free.

My dad doesn't approve of me (DK)

He never asked his dad, so he didn't really know what his dad thought, regardless of how he interpreted his dad's actions.

...and never will (DK)

A prediction about his father in the future.

I lack whatever it takes to make him proud of me (DK)

He had no idea what it took to make his father proud, because he never asked.

I have to keep trying (F)

He might want to keep trying, but he certainly doesn't have to.

I have to keep proving to him that I'm worthwhile (F)

The 'have to' makes it F, and you can never prove your worth-while-ness enough to make that demand go away. There is always some incident your mind can focus on to prove your unworthiness. At the spiritual level, your very being is enough to prove your worthiness – you are a vessel of life, and that's enough.

I'm missing something (F)

He was missing nothing. That was the only thing his mind could come up with that would explain his father's reaction.

I don't know what it is (T)

He couldn't know what it was, because he wasn't missing anything.

So whatever I'm missing can never get fixed (F)

There was nothing to fix.

I'm never gonna win here, not really (DK)

A prediction about his father, and how Life will be with his father, that he is really clueless about.

It's hopeless for me (F)

There is always hope.

The gang member's Lifeshock and mindtalk:

Lifeshock: seeing his little sister crying brokenly, for the third time.

Reaction/feelings: sick > stomach; scared > gut

Mindtalk:

I can't do anything (F)

Obviously this one is F. Even at 12 there were loads of things he could do.

He (the step-father) is going to kill me (DK)

It's a statement about the future, could have been a possibility, but definitely not known for sure.

He hates me (DK)

The stepfather never said that, and even though he wasn't a teddy bear kind of guy, he could have felt lots of different ways about his stepson.

I'm no good anyway (F)

One of those judgments about his BEING that was totally false.

I can't even protect my sisters (F)

'I can't' infers 'physically unable' – which most of the time is false. In fact, upon further investigation as we did the Clarity Process, he revealed that he actually did protect his sisters, hiding them when he could.

I have to get out of here (F)

He didn't 'have to' get out of there; some don't. He wanted to get out of there.

I can't make it on the streets on my own (DK)

Another statement about the future. Some kids do make it on the streets, some don't.

I'm weak and powerless (F) (F)

Both are judgments, both F, because they are statements about his BEING. He may not have been strong and powerful compared to his stepfather, but that does not rob him of the strength and power he did have as a 12-year-old.

The only safe harbor is to become a gang member (F)

Becoming a gang member is not a 'safe harbor' – and certainly not the 'only one.' When we are scared, the possibilities of other options rarely come to mind. Going to a relative, to a school counselor, pastor/priest, even the police – those don't even register when the prevailing option in the neighborhood is the gang.

They will protect me (DK)

Another statement about the future, and definitely a DK about whether they will protect him or not.

I have to join a gang (F)

Another demand that closes down possibility, definitely F.

… or I'll die (DK)

This is a prediction about the future, and he also hooked the fear of dying to having to join a gang, which would make it a double DK. Joining a gang is anything but a guaranteed protection from dying. (In one sense, we all die eventually, and if he had said it that way, it would have been true.)

My Lifeshock and mindtalk:

Lifeshock: seeing a black body bag being wheeled through the front door on a gurney.

Reaction/feelings: shocked > whole torso; immobilized > all over

Mindtalk:

This isn't happening (F)

It was happening.

She can't be dead (F)

We had known her disease was terminal for ten years, but in OUR reality, a cure was going to be discovered any day, and Susie would be saved. But this wasn't a dream; she really was dead. So My reality was in conflict with the Real Reality, which reigns supreme.

I have to make this un-happen (F)

I actually can't do that.

This isn't right (F)

This is a tough one. 'Right' is entirely subjective; it's literally my judgment, which is not the same as The Truth. In reality, I don't have the objectivity to know what is 'right' and what is 'wrong.' If I were looking at this from Susie's point of view, I suspect she would think it was 'right' – finally.

This doesn't happen in my family (F)

It happens in all families eventually.

I didn't stop it (T)

I didn't know how to stop her dying; neither did the medical profession.

I should have known what to do (F)

That was a demand that assumes omnipotence.

This is happening way too fast (F)

'Too fast' is another judgment. It was actually happening at the pace that it was happening. I wanted it to be different. It wasn't.

I need to slow things down (F)

I don't 'need' to do anything. And in this case, there was no way for me slow things down to a speed at which I would have been comfortable.

I can't handle all this (F)

I wasn't handling this Lifeshock in a gracious way, but I was handling it the way I did; which in retrospect, given that there was no rehearsal, was supportive of my other brothers and sisters and my parents.

... because I'm incompetent and stupid (F) (F)

I am neither of those accusations. I am not totally competent and smart in every situation, but I am competent and smart.

I have to pretend this never happened (F)

I don't have to be enslaved in a pretense of something that is simply not reality.

I had a more than passing acquaintance with this string of mindtalk. I can't remember when I didn't think that I should have it all handled and know what to do at all times. As the eldest of eight, it came naturally. It all sounds so normal, that the only way I can tell I am victimizing myself is by the feelings of shock and/or desperation in my body. That's when I go back and look for the Lifeshock, feel my feelings, listen to the mindtalk, and verify what is T, F, or DK.

Chapter 6

Telling the Truth

Telling the Truth, the Real Truth, starts the whole freeing process, which elicits my creativity and productivity. It also synchronizes my reality with The Reality, which grants all kinds of possibilities that are not there when I'm trying to re-shape The Reality to fit into My reality.

There is a quick, efficient way to complete the next part of the Clarity Process, and then there is a deeper, more intense way. *in step 4)*

The quick and efficient way, is to look back over what you have done so far: Identifying the Lifeshock, re-experiencing it with your senses plugged in, feeling your feelings, listening to the mindtalk, writing it all down, and then going back and verifying each separate statement as T, F, or DK. Let yourself be suspicious of any statement that you have marked with a T. Double-check it; is it actually 100% true? Two things are always true about a Lifeshock: the Lifeshock itself, what really happened, is true; and how you felt is true. And there may be other Ts that were a part of your mindtalk. Notice all the Fs and DKs, but in the quick, efficient way, *in* you'll write down only those things that were real and true *step* about the Lifeshock itself. *9*

The deeper, more intense way to do the truth-telling takes more time, but it can have a longer-lasting effect. This is especially good when we have had the same kind of mindtalk for several Clarity processes. It puts the lies to bed in a more irrefutable way. In this case, not only is it important to write down all the truths of the Lifeshock – what happened, the feelings, any Ts in the mindtalk – but also to write at least one full sentence or paragraph about what is true for each statement marked F and DK. (This is what I did for the verifications in the previous chapter.) For those really tough lies, it's helpful to write a whole paragraph about what is true. By the end of this part of the Clarity Process, you will have a list of truths that can be a foundation for believing in yourself and behaving in ways that are congruent with yourself when you are at your best. It's like having your own personal scripture, won the hard way.

In the physician's process, the bare-bones truth was that he was expecting his dad to behave in specific ways. In his case, he expected a proud dad to give lots of verbal approval. Verbal approval = being loved (in the physician's mind). What was also true is that he had never told his dad what he wanted, nor had he ever asked his dad how he felt about him.

If the physician had told more extensive truths, he would have admitted that he didn't really need his father's approval in order to feel fulfilled or to believe in himself. It was also true that, in fact, he never really needed to prove anything to anyone – ever. Not Really. The truth was that he was an honorable, loving son, brother, husband, father who loved his life and wanted to make a difference in the lives of others. The truth was that he had been gifted with intelligence, an athletic/robust body, good looks, a gentle heart, and loving parents. The truth was that he was lacking nothing, really. The truth was he felt grateful for all his gifts. He saw how well positioned he was to give back to the world at large – not out of proving or seeking approval, but out of gratitude for the quality of his life – one into which he was born, and which he continued to hone.

In the gang member's process, what was true was he saw his little sister crying for the third time. It was true that he felt sick and scared. Nothing else was true. Discovering the extent of the lies he was telling himself was a total shock. He realized that he had based the whole rest of his life on things a 12-year-old made up, none of which were true.

Had he done more extensive verification, he might have discovered more significant truths about himself, like:

I wanted to protect my sisters from being abused.

I was 12, not a physical match for my stepfather.

I didn't know how to stop the abuse.

I didn't know there were other possibilities, so I didn't even search.

I love my sisters. I want them to be treated with love and respect and with gentleness.

I care deeply about my family.

I matter – to myself, to my sisters, and to others.

I want my family to be loving and respectful of each other.

Truthfully, I am sensitive to those I love.

I'm not 12 now.

In my process, what was true was seeing the black body bag being wheeled out our front door. It was true I felt shock in my torso and immobilized/frozen all over. There was one statement in my mindtalk that was true: *I didn't stop it.*
Here are my truths about the rest of the Fs and DKs.

Death is a natural part of living, part of the cycle of life. I don't want to dishonor or be afraid of any part of that cycle.
There have been and likely will be more instances where I won't know what to do. I don't have to know what to do in every instance. I can trust myself to respond to each moment with all that I am and all I can bring at that time. I know what I know, and that is enough.

Life unfolds in its own time. I have no control over the fastness or slowness with which it does that. I don't even want the control. I want to keep participating as fully as possible, bringing my best to each moment, whether I like what's happening or not. I trust myself, and I trust Life.

I did handle that moment and all the moments before and after. I was in my 20s. I would likely have handled it differently had I been 10 or 30.

Chapter 7

Choosing Consciously

This next part of the Clarity Process is the point of change – the point of being proactive in our own lives. This is where our lives can change in a conscious way – breaking out of our illusion of imprisonment (drivenness, proving, victimhood, martyrdom, etc.) and becoming more aligned with our goodness, our passion, our destiny.

Usually there is so much relief from shucking the lies that the temptation is to rest in the solace. Often we feel so much more energy and clarity that we get caught up in our renewed vitality and stop there.

The purpose of the first four steps – re-experiencing the Lifeshock, listening to our mindtalk, verifying what's T, F, DK, and telling the truth – is to deliver us to the point where we make proactive, conscious choices that address the more destructive pieces of mindtalk. What will we stop doing that gets us into this deceptive spin, and what will we start doing that moves us forward to claiming our dreams?

All the previous actions clear out the rubbish generated in the reactive mind and are in support of this next step – consciously choosing the quality of our lives.

From the previous examples, here are what some choices were:

The physician:
He chose to stop the old program of expecting his dad (or anyone) to show him approval. (This kind of choice usually takes some conscious herding to bring to fruition.)

He also chose to ask his dad for some private time, to tell him what it was like for him to not have overt approval and what he made up about his dad's lack of demonstrativeness, and see what his dad had to say (without having to have his approval).

The gang member:

His first choice was to talk to his sisters. He wasn't 12 years old anymore, but he wanted them to know that he was there for them in all the ways he could be.

His second choice was to re-frame himself as a man, not an impotent boy going up against Goliath (his step-father). In that context, he could make decisions based on his real age.

My choice:

My choices were to talk about Susie, especially with family members. I also committed to hanging the pictures of her and me in my home.

For three and a half years I volunteered at a hospital's Stage 4 cancer ward, engaging with people who were either dying or fighting the good fight, or both. Those patients allowed me to learn about living, even as they were dying. I learned from them what I refused to learn from Susie.

*****

To make conscious choices, ask yourself:
- What will I stop doing/being?
- What will I start doing/being?
- How will I be WHILE I do what I do?

A popular choice is to commit to using the Clarity Process several times a week – just to keep the decks clear.

As a friend of mine said, the Clarity Process is like mental floss – it gets the detritus out from between the brain cells.

Tip:
Promises made when making a choice, if not kept, often result in a Lifeshock for another Clarity Process, until personal resistance to change is eventually worn down.

Chapter 8

Visualizing

Visualization is the initiation of conscious change in our lives. If we cannot even imagine the new choice taking effect, being brought into reality, its chance of actually happening is slim to none. So to test the viability of our choices, it is important to be able to visualize the successful manifestation of any commitment we make.

This is where the impact of the reticular activating system (RAS) can truly enhance the quality of our lives. There are two things that energize the RAS – first, a mental image that is acute with sensory data, everything you see, hear, smell, taste, touch (feel on your skin); and second, the concomitant feelings, physical sensations in your body. The more specific the image, the more detail you see, hear, smell, taste, touch. The greater the feelings that go with that, the more likelihood your RAS will research the field of possibilities and pay attention to those doors which will offer the realization of your dreams. And there are no guarantees – absolutely none, ever. of success –

The important bit to remember is that engaging your RAS in an image that is consciously chosen, as in the fifth step of "Choose now what to do," electrifying it with sensory data and heightened feelings, sending it out into the limitless field of possibilities, and being curious about what happens next – that is a high game to play all on its own.

Example:
The physician imagined himself asking for some private time with his dad. He pictured himself being whole and complete in himself, trusting himself, feeling grateful for the gifts his dad had given him, then seeing himself asking if his dad was proud of him.

Example:
The gang member pictured himself as a grown man, fully able to take charge of his own life, strong, caring about his sisters, telling them how much he loved them, and how, even at the age of 12, he did what he could to protect them.

Example:
I visualized myself talking with my family, telling Susie stories, feeling at peace, connected with her, grateful for her impact in my life.

Hint – the RAS can be used to keep our focus on how we want to be in the future, what we want our future to look like, be like.

I've focused my RAS on a future image that feels compelling for me. It looks like this:
I am 80 years old, mentally aware, fit in body, spiritually at peace, walking around a compound where all my family and best mates live – a conscious community of like-hearted souls. I'm wearing a belted skirt and tunic, relishing the clean air, the smell of the orchards, the cool shade of the trees. My posture is erect and flexible, my eyes are clear and bright, a Mona Lisa smile tugs my lips. I first hear then see a gaggle of kids running in my direction. They swirl around me, laughing, knowing that I care about them and see them at their finest and settle for nothing less. I feel delight in their innocence, proud of what I've been a part of in my life and theirs. Grateful tears sting my eyes. My heart swells open even more.

Quantum physics experiments (The Intention Experiment by Lynne McTaggart) have begun testing the power of intention, which has visualization at its core. However, many already know the effectiveness of visualization, hence the popularity of vision boards.

Visualizations generated by fear (worry, desperation, resignation, hopelessness, revenge, victimhood, martyrdom, depression, rage, coldness, etc.) are also powerful and draw us toward the scary doors that are also open to us. It's not up to our RAS to distinguish between our wanted and unwanted images. That is our right to choose; we have free will. It is our mastery that is at stake.

If we are feeling any emotion that separates us from our best self or from others or from the sense of being in the flow of life, we are at the effect of some belief that is a lie. There will be a Lifeshock we said NO to that started the chain of mindtalk that now has our RAS working overtime to spot those doors that open to our personal wormholes. It's up to us to recognize our own dis-ease and to course-correct.

Chapter 9

Lifeshocks – Our Teacher

Lifeshocks will pester us until we wake up. If pestering doesn't get it, Lifeshocks will bang on our self-imposed prison until we cannot ignore the wake-up call any longer – or until we are dead. Even then I wonder if Lifeshocks abate or if they change form to suit whatever the post-dead state requires for evolution.

I knew of a young man in college who had a lump under his arm. He was scared of what it might be, so he ignored it, pretending he couldn't feel it or see it. His mother noticed it one day when he took off his shirt. She took him to the doctor immediately. By that time, the tumor was so big that the cancer had spread to other parts of his body, and he died within a few months. There is no guarantee that he would have lived if he had checked out that lump in the early stages. But likely the scenario would have played out much differently had he done that.

In the early '80s, When I went to the Life Training Weekend, now called the More To Life Weekend, I was quite satisfied with my life. When that woman stepped into her own nobility, I was inspired to step more into mine.

Lifeshocks abound. They are never not present. They either are accepted or resisted. They insist that we evolve and mature and bloom, while still giving us the option to stay stuck, act like spoiled brats, and/or wither before our time.

Lifeshocks have three faces. One face, Exposing Lifeshocks, wakes us up to be our best, to our personal mastery, personal accountability, personal ethics, being real, standing for who we are, illuminating our dreams, expressing our uniqueness, restoring our hope for our lives. Should we decide otherwise, Life is quick to send us Lifeshocks that wake us up to our personal betrayal of our essential self, exposing our pretense of being more, or less, than we really are.

The second face, Evoking Lifeshocks, is the face of relationships – all relationships, including our relationship with Mother Earth. These Lifeshocks evoke our compassion, our connections with each other, our ability to love others and to allow in the love from others. When we get into isolation, competition, resentment, or game-playing, Life will be right there with some Lifeshock that calls us into our commonness, our relatedness, our 'for-ness' for each other – including each of us holding all of us accountable (tough love).

The third face of Lifeshocks, Limiting Lifeshocks, pertains to being in right relationship with the big 'R' Reality, which includes living within the limits set by big 'R' Reality. It has many names: God, Allah, The Force, Universal Light, The Divine One, Higher Power, Life, Supreme BEING, just to name a few. Held within that big 'R' Reality are many lesser dimensions of reality. This third face of Lifeshocks can address any bigger context in which we find ourselves – our culture, gender, school, place of worship, workplace, other cultures, our country, planet, solar system, universe. We do not have the power to impose our limits on those bigger contexts. In fact, just the reverse. There is a reality to those bigger contexts that puts us in our place, humbles us, reminds us of who's who in the universe. These Limiting Lifeshocks wake us up to our humanity, our humbleness, to the unpopular truth that we are not in charge. We are not omniscient, it is not up to us to fix everything, make it all right, or save the world. These Lifeshocks summon our faith – faith that, in some incomprehensible way, all is well. Always. Including contexts that we want to be a part of changing.

We influence contexts, just by being in one. Part of being faith-full is knowing that all contexts in which we find ourselves are exactly the ones in which we have the opportunity to evolve, as well as to be a part of evolving that context.

Faith, hope and love – that's what Lifeshocks are offering us, teaching us, relentlessly presenting. When we fall out of love, sink into hopelessness, lose our faith, Lifeshocks will be there. Once we let go of the gross lies, Life will be there, sending the more subtle Lifeshocks, awakening us even further. There is always more – more to let go of, more to be, more life even richer in faith, hope, and love.

In the Christian tradition, these three faces of Lifeshocks correspond to wake-up messages from God the Father, the Creator (Limiting Lifeshocks, Faith); God the Son, the Redeemer (Exposing Lifeshocks, Hope); and God the Holy Spirit, the Sanctifier (Evoking Lifeshocks, Love). In the Jewish culture, the messages are from YHWH (Limiting), the prophets (Exposing), the Covenant (Evoking). The Hindu tradition has Brahma (Limiting), Vishnu (Exposing), Shiva (Evoking). I'm guessing that most religions have representations of the faces of Lifeshocks. The comics have Lucy – Limiting (taking away the football), Charlie Brown – Exposing (learning about himself), and Snoopy – Evoking (surrounded by the little birds). Great literature often is a recounting of the lessons of faith, hope, and love as delivered by the various Lifeshocks in the story. Those messages reverberate within us and call us forward.

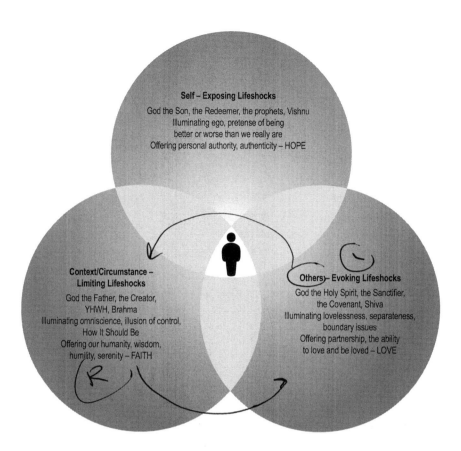

Self – Exposing Lifeshocks
God the Son, the Redeemer, the prophets, Vishnu
Illuminating ego, pretense of being better or worse than we really are
Offering personal authority, authenticity – HOPE

Others – Evoking Lifeshocks
God the Holy Spirit, the Sanctifier, the Covenant, Shiva
Illuminating lovelessness, separateness, boundary issues
Offering partnership, the ability to love and be loved – LOVE

Context/Circumstance – Limiting Lifeshocks

God the Father, the Creator, YHWH, Brahma
Illuminating omniscience, illusion of control, How It Should Be
Offering our humanity, wisdom, humility, serenity – FAITH

The point of this Venn diagram is to stand in the middle of the confluence of the three frames of reference – Self, Others, Context/Circumstance – and be aware of the Lifeshocks in each. For instance, I have an intention to record three Lifeshocks daily. I also record whether each Lifeshock is Exposing my pretense, inviting more of my authenticity; Evoking my love-ability, inviting me to let go of my isolation; or Limiting my omniscience, inviting more of my humanity – or any combination of the three.

I've noticed that I often get a preponderance of one kind of Lifeshock (usually Limiting), which tells me that I'm being offered an opportunity to choose to course-correct in that area. In the case of Limiting Lifeshocks, to get off my need to "fix things" (believing it's up to me to make things "right" – my version of "right," of course). When I say yes to the Limiting Lifeshock, I am offered the gift of serenity (the wisdom to know what I can/can't change).

Those circles are rarely in a state of perfect balance. Normally one or the other is being emphasized. If my child is sick, the "Other" circle becomes paramount. If I have a deadline at work, the "Context/Circumstance" circle looms larger. However, if my "Context/Circumstance" circle habitually consumes most of my energy, and the "Self" circle stays small, I will get Lifeshocks about that, often physical disorders. If I don't course-correct, the Lifeshocks will get bigger, often from family members – begging for more time, etc. The Lifeshocks will continue to come, even after I've course-corrected, calling me into more creativity, productivity, love-ability, connection, wisdom, serenity, personal authority, authenticity, and realness.

Recording Lifeshocks is a great way to monitor the degree of our awake-ness in each circle. It doesn't take much time, and it's revealing of the quality of our lives Now. We are worth monitoring our own lives. We can abdicate responsibility for that, which requires others to monitor our behavior, which eventually they will. And we probably won't like it. Recording your Lifeshocks is a simple way to take radical responsibility for your own life. Pay attention to the Lifeshocks, course-correct, go for it again … repeat.

Chapter 10

Gifts of Life

I was driving from Boulder to Keystone, Colorado, alone in my Subaru Outback (great mountain-climbing car), plugging in my new Barbra Streisand CD, feeling a little sorry for myself (don't remember why). The Rocky Mountains are huge. My mindtalk interpreted their immensity as further proof that I was insignificant, of no consequence, just another piece of flotsam on the ocean of humanity. (Yep, downright pathetic.)

With this as the background, the CD started. I'd never heard it before. The first cut is *I Believe/You'll Never Walk Alone*. This song was meant for me at that specific time. The second cut, *Higher Ground*, took me to my knees figuratively. My throat ached, hot tears made rivulets down my face, my nose ran, my chest felt too small to contain the swelling of raw feeling that was released in me. Now the Rockies seemed to reassure me that they had seen it all. In the grand scheme of things, *I* was not insignificant – my problems were insignificant. Bottom line, the Lifeshock of the lyrics, interpreted as above, lifted me out of the doldrums and into gratitude.

And in the grand scheme of things, all is well ... ALL is well. There is no way to mess up this human existence. When we fall short of our innate goodness, or withhold our charity to others, or wallow in our faithlessness, Life, in all of its beneficence, will send us a Lifeshock to course-correct our fall from grace or evolve us further down our path. Should we persist in our ego-driven demands that we be different than we are, that others be different than they are, or that Life be different that It Is, Life, in all of its beneficence, will increase the amplitude of the Lifeshocks until we cannot NOT get the message.

If we habituate ourselves to our yucky-ness, having our spoiled-brat meltdowns (which includes the silent withdrawal of energy), we become the warning to everyone else about how not to be. Life will still use us as Lifeshocks to everyone else about the consequences of saying NO to the Way IT IS.

I don't have to like the Way IT IS in order to say YES to it. In fact, that's usually how change begins. The scale says 160 lbs. I don't like that, AND that's the Way IT IS . . . for now. Or I could say NO, the scale is wrong, and continue to indulge my fantasy life, increasing the possibility of the scale trending upwards.

Does this mean that we have to say YES to everything and capitulate to the Way IT IS, even if the Way IT IS is unjust or out of integrity or demeaning?

The point is to say YES – that's how it is, and here's what I want to do about that.

Sometimes there is nothing to do but accept that Life is different than I thought. And sometimes those incidents lead to more global course-corrections, like after giant oil spills. Dwelling in our righteous NO changes nothing, except to deepen our neural network's groove into impotence (because we don't have the power to un-happen what has happened). Sometimes it's a matter of admitting that the ethics of our workplace are not in alignment with our personal ethics. We don't have to change the company; we can change our workplace. And if we want, we can be an initiator of change in our company. Saying YES to Reality is simply admitting how It Really Is – which increases our capability to be response-able – able to respond consciously to the real lay of the land and make choices that are congruent with the best in us.

There are so many holy books and so much spiritually inspiring literature that call forth our authentic self, that humble our ego, that awaken us to possibilities and dreams that are sacred ... and scary. Scary because, once I admit how much something matters, there is an accountability to mySelf that requires focus, energy to manifest that dream. Then the battle begins. Do I have what it takes to manifest my dreams? My reactive mind usually says, "No way!" My creative mind says, "Who knows? And I WANT to go for it."

Either road we choose, whether we go for it or settle for our habitual behavior, there are no guarantees. Life is not predictable. The reactive mind insists on predictability, which it equates to safety. Each moment, each breath of our life, is a step into the unknown. When we exhale, when we let go of our breath, trusting the next breath will be there (and being OK if it's not), we feel the excitement, the challenge of partnering with Life itself. Admittedly, it's easier when we like the Lifeshocks we're getting. And ultimately, the choice is ours – always ours: Live in a little personal reality parallel to the Real one, or live in the Real Reality. There are consequences either way – and no guarantees either way.

CHAPTER 11

What's Possible Now?

My hope is that this book gives us yet another way to make continuous course-corrections that are conscious and worthy of the best in us, choices that serve our personal and common destinies.

Learning to recognize Lifeshocks and using the Clarity Process to stay current in our own evolution are cornerstones of the More To Life program. Additional components include processes covering the following:

- Saying what we mean, meaning what we say
- Uncovering and releasing hidden or long-term negativity
- Reclaiming our personal authority
- Deepening our connection to our own essence
- Letting go of the resentment and walls between ourselves and others, true forgiveness
- Making peace with ourselves, getting off our own back
- Using our RAS in a personal strategic plan to produce the results we want in our lives

The More To Life program is now worldwide. Besides the More To Life Weekend, which is led by Senior Trainer(s), there are 3 other entry-level courses taught by Mentors, as well as 11 weekend courses focused on some aspect of the human experience, and 8 week-long residential courses. Some of these courses have been taught in the United States, the United Kingdom, South Africa, New Zealand, Australia, Germany, Spain, France, Monaco, Italy, Kuwait, Colombia, Mexico, Jordan, Iceland, China, and I don't know where else. There are students of the program who have become Mentors, Coaches, Consultants, and Trainers, spreading the principles and tools of the program wherever they go.

If any of this interests you, visit the More To Life website at www.moretolife ~~.org~~ US. ovg
You can also catch me on my *Life As It Is* blog at http://www.annmcmaster.com.

Following are some stories from people who have participated in the More To Life program, as they recall how the program has impacted their lives.

COMPENDIUM OF STORIES

Pam, North Carolina

I'm 51 years old. I've been married twenty-four years and I have two children, ages 17½ and 13. In the last few years I've witnessed several of my friends' marriages fall apart. From the outside looking in (and with limited knowledge), I see how resentment, anger, and fear have taken their toll on these relationships.

I took the More To Life Weekend (then called the Life Training Weekend) about twenty-six years ago. My husband has taken it, too. As I count my blessings for my family and the relationship I have with each of them, I often wonder if it is the tools and wisdom gained from the Weekend that have helped us maintain our love and respect for each other.

Don't get me wrong. We are not perfect. Our love is not without issues. We have our moments, to be sure. But we also both have the language to let the other person know when we aren't telling the truth or living in our personal power and integrity. I know how to express how my mind is tricking me and ask for help in clearing through to the truth. My children, having been raised with this, are AMAZING at calling me on my stuff when my mindtalk takes over. Nothing snaps me back to myself faster than my own child pointing out my mindtalk.

When my old dramas and guiding beliefs grab hold after a particularly juicy Lifeshock and I tell myself lies about myself, including how unworthy and unlovable I am, I use an abbreviated version of the Clarity Process to look around, tell the truth about myself and the situation, and make clear choices. I've had plenty of opportunities to look at Lifeshocks now that my children are older. My mind can run rampant with anxiety, wondering if we are doing all the right things to ensure their happiness and success, or if the choices they make now will ruin their chances for a good future. I use the tools of More To Life to notice my fear and anxiety, and the mindtalk that's fueling it.

I would like to believe that ONE DAY my old beliefs and mindtalk will disappear but, as yet, that hasn't happened. When I'm particularly down emotionally, I will revert to my old dramas of thinking I don't fit in, that I am not good enough, that something is wrong with me. But I don't stay there nearly as long as I used to. I am able to see much quicker how my mind got the best of me and say, "Oh, okay, there it is again," and then be honest about the situation that I'm stressed about.

I don't mean to use other people's misery to my advantage, but when I do see my friends who have divorced or have unhappy marriages or relationships, I see what I think could have been me had I not had the tools to tell the truth about who I really am. Before the Weekend, and even for some time afterward, my M.O. was to push people away before they could find out who 'I really was.' I believe what I learned from the More To Life program has allowed me to love and be loved, and to live life with gratitude and joy (most of the time!).

P.A.K., Founder and CEO of a software company, USA

Since about the age of 10 I have been very uncomfortable with heights. In 2004 I was at a More To Life course and did a Clarity Process on this feeling. What I found, as I felt the feelings associated with heights, was a traumatic event at about age 9 that was at the root of this issue – the death of my dog at the bottom of a cliff.

As I did the Clarity Process, I filled a page with all my mindtalk related to that incident and how high places result in death. When I came back to the present moment in the class, I was looking at all this mindtalk, and it became clear how this past event had such a strong hold on me. I went through each line, verifying with a vengeance the falseness of it all. At the end I had my Truth: "This event happened to me as a young boy and left its mark on me." The rest were all false statements that I made up in my mind.

I chose to claim reality whenever I looked down from a high position. It sounds something like: "This place and time are not the one I experienced at age 9!" Soon after that Clarity Process I was able to enjoy a ride on a high zip-line in Costa Rica. Today, more than 10 years later, I can look down from our balcony on the 24th floor and enjoy the sand and ocean below. I am not ready to walk on the railing or do a tightrope walk. But then I did not do that before the traumatic event when I was 9, either.

Linda, South Dakota

I took what was then called The Life Training Weekend because some friends of mine from Kodak were going to the Weekend, and I had such respect for these women that I thought if they believed it was a good course, then it 'must be.'

I knew for myself that I wanted more contentment and happiness in my life. Something seemed to be missing, so I said 'yes' to going to the course, hoping it would add to my life.

One of the biggest things that I got from the Weekend was a willingness to be vulnerable. Before the course I had a drama about 'my life is fine' and 'I'm always okay.' What an awakening for me – to not pretend I was okay.

I did not believe I was loveable or very capable. And, until the course, I didn't know that it was okay to love yourself. With the help of the Clarity Process I learned that I am enough, I don't have to live my life as a victim, and I am not a victim.

How has the Weekend changed my life? My relationships, especially with my children and husband, are enriched. We are closer than we have ever been. I am more open and honest with them. I am truly grateful for the More To Life program. And I still have a support partner and use the processes. They are a big part of my life.

Made in the USA
San Bernardino, CA
12 January 2015